Herbie the Love Bug The Lovable, Curious, Sometimes Naughty Dachshund

Written and designed by Brandi Brandt

©2023 by Brandi Brandt

Printed in the United States of America

Published in Hellertown, PA

Cover and interior design by Brandi Brandt

Library of Congress Control Number: 2023907234

ISBN: 978-1-958711-47-7

For more information or to place bulk orders, contact the author at brandilady@gmail.com.

INSPIRED BY MY LOVE FOR DACHSHUNDS

To my daughter, Jamie, "I hope you dance."
To my son, Jared, "As long as I'm living, my baby you'll be."
To my husband, Bud, "But what if you fly?"
To my niece, Olivia, "Shine your light in this world."

4

Hi! My name is Herbie the Love Bug.
I'm not a bug though.
I'm a dachshund puppy.

What is your name?
Are you ready to learn a little bit about me?

Did you know?
The most popular dog
names in 2022 were
Charlie, Bella, Daisy,
Milo, Lucy, Buddy,
and Lily.

May 31st is my birthday. When I was born, my dog mommy had four other puppies. I have two brothers and two sisters. I spent the first eight weeks in the world with them. In that time, I learned to walk, eat, wag my tail, and even bark!

When is your birthday?
What kind of things did you
learn when you were small?
Do you have any brothers or
sisters?

Did you know?
The average litter
size of the
dachshunds is one
to six puppies.

After eight weeks with my dog mommy,
I went home with my human mommy
and daddy. They adopted me. Adopted
means that they provided me a home to live
in with a warm bed, food, and lots of love.
I love living with my human mommy
and daddy.

*Does your home have a
warm bed, food, and lots
of love?*

Did you know?
Adopting a puppy can reduce
stress, anxiety and depression,
and it encourages exercise,
ultimately, improving your
all-around health.

I like my new home.
I've been doing
a lot of exploring.
Mommy says I am so curious
about everything.
There are so many new smells,
sounds, tastes, and sights.
I think one of my favorite
smells is flowers.

What is your
favorite smell?

Did you know?
A dog can smell
objects and people
up to 12 miles away.

Right now my mommy and daddy are trying to train me to go potty outside. When I do go potty outside, I get a treat. I'm learning to go potty outside,
but sometimes I have accidents and go potty on the floor in the house. When that happens,
my mommy and daddy remind me that I need
to go potty outside.
I'm really trying hard to go potty outside all of the time, especially because I like treats!

*Are there things that you try really
hard to learn?*

Did you know?
It typically takes
four to six months
to fully potty train
a puppy.

As I got older, I liked to chew on things,
and I got in trouble a couple of times.
One day, I pulled the threads
out of my mommy's carpet.
My mommy told me in a very stern voice
that I was not allowed to put things in my
mouth that were not mine. Then she gave
me a toy to chew on and reminded me that
I'm only allowed to chew on my toys.

*Did you ever get in trouble for
doing something you weren't
supposed to do?*

Did you know?
Just like human babies,
puppies teething and
chewing on things makes
their gums feel better.

Look
how big
I got!

Some puppies are big, and some are little. Some are really tall, and some are really short.
Just like humans.
We are all born in our own special way.
My mommy says that when I was born, I was the size of a peach. Now that I'm full grown,
she says I'm as long as a snake!
In fact, as dachshunds puppies grow, they get longer! Some people call us "hot dogs"
because we are so long.
I don't think that is very funny though.
I don't want anyone to think they can eat me!

Do you know how tall you are?
Have you ever seen a dachshund like me?

Did you know?
The longest dachshund
recorded was nearly
three feet long!

I love to eat!
I eat all of my breakfast in the morning
and all of my dinner in the evening,
and sometimes I'm still hungry!
When my mommy and daddy eat,
I make my eyes look sad
so they want to share their food with me.
Some of my favorite snacks are bananas,
carrots, beef jerky, bacon, and peanut
butter.

What are some of your
favorite snacks?

Did you know?
Studies show that
dogs can
communicate to their
owners to get what
they want.

I love going for walks! I get super excited
when I see my mommy get my leash.
My mommy says that walking is
exercise, and exercise keeps me healthy.
On our walks, I move my little legs fast
and sniff everything I can.
Sometimes we see other doggies while
walking,
and I get to stop and say hi to them.
Walking makes me feel so good.
It must be because it makes me healthy.

*What are your favorite
exercises?*

Did you know?
Walks benefit dogs by providing
mental stimulation, exercise,
and socialization.

I like to play a lot. I like to try to get my mommy and daddy to chase me through the house.
I usually take their socks or shoes and run with them!
They chase me and yell, "Get back here with that, Herbie!"
It's really funny!

What kind of games do you like to play?

Did you know?
Some fun games to play with a dog are tug of war, hide and seek, and fetch.

I don't like to take baths! I get my baths in the kitchen sink. As soon as I get wet, I try to jump out of the sink. My mommy and daddy need to hold me down to shampoo me.
They say I need a bath because I get dirty and start to smell stinky.
Once bath time is over, my mommy dries me off, and I get really energized! I run all over the house super duper fast!
My mommy and daddy say that I get the "zoomies."

Do you ever get super energized and get the zoomies like me?

Did you know?
Dogs only need a bath
every two to three
months.

Bedtime is my favorite time of the day.
My mommy and daddy put me
in their bed to sleep.
I like to cuddle in my mommy's favorite blanket.
Mommy and Daddy pet me
and give me lots of kisses, and they say,
"Night night, Herbie. We love you."
And I fall right to sleep.

*What are the things that you do
to get ready for bed?*

Did you know?
Dogs have dreams just like
humans do.

I really hope you liked
learning about me!
I hope we can have
more fun together soon!

Herbie
The Love Bug

About the Author

Brandi Brandt is a recent empty nester of two adult children. But before her heart became completely deflated, she was blessed with the adoption of Herbie, her little love bug.

Now with her husband and furry crew of three, the laughter never stops in their home.

She hopes to provide a portion of their fun with the world, by sharing a small fraction of the their daily doggy shenanigans. She looks forward to writing more books about her furry family.

CPSIA information can be obtained
at www.ICGtesting.com
Printed in the USA
BVHW011320040523
663580BV00019B/911